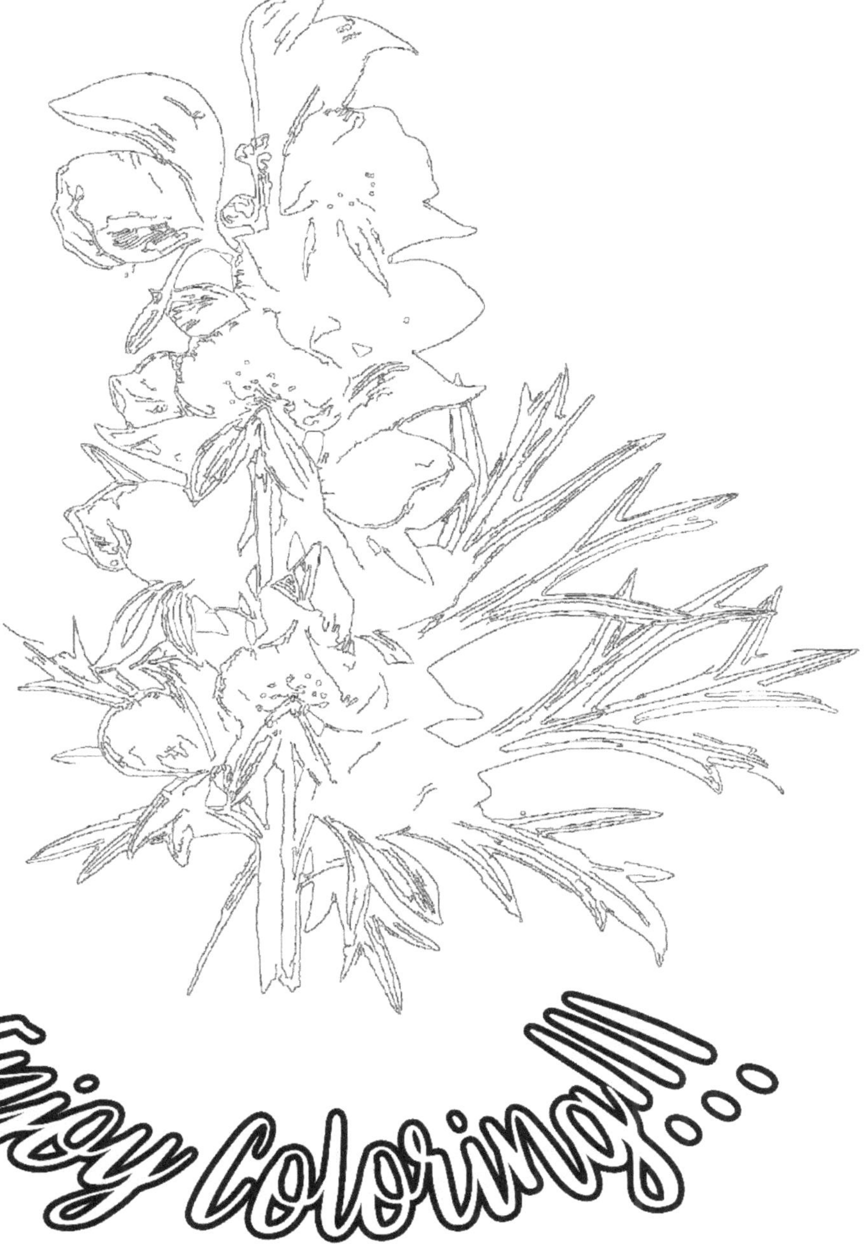

Enjoy Coloring!!!...

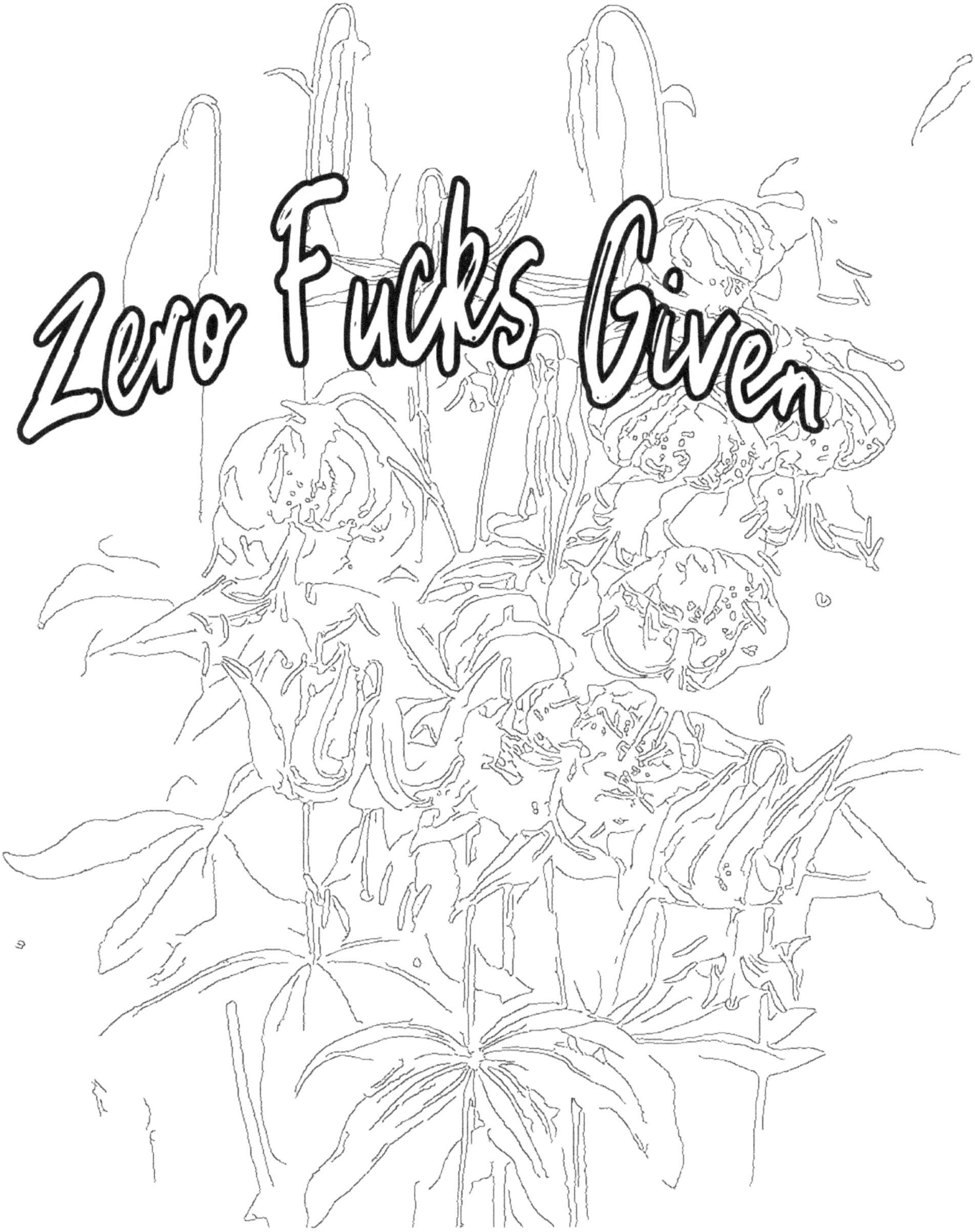
Zero Fucks Given

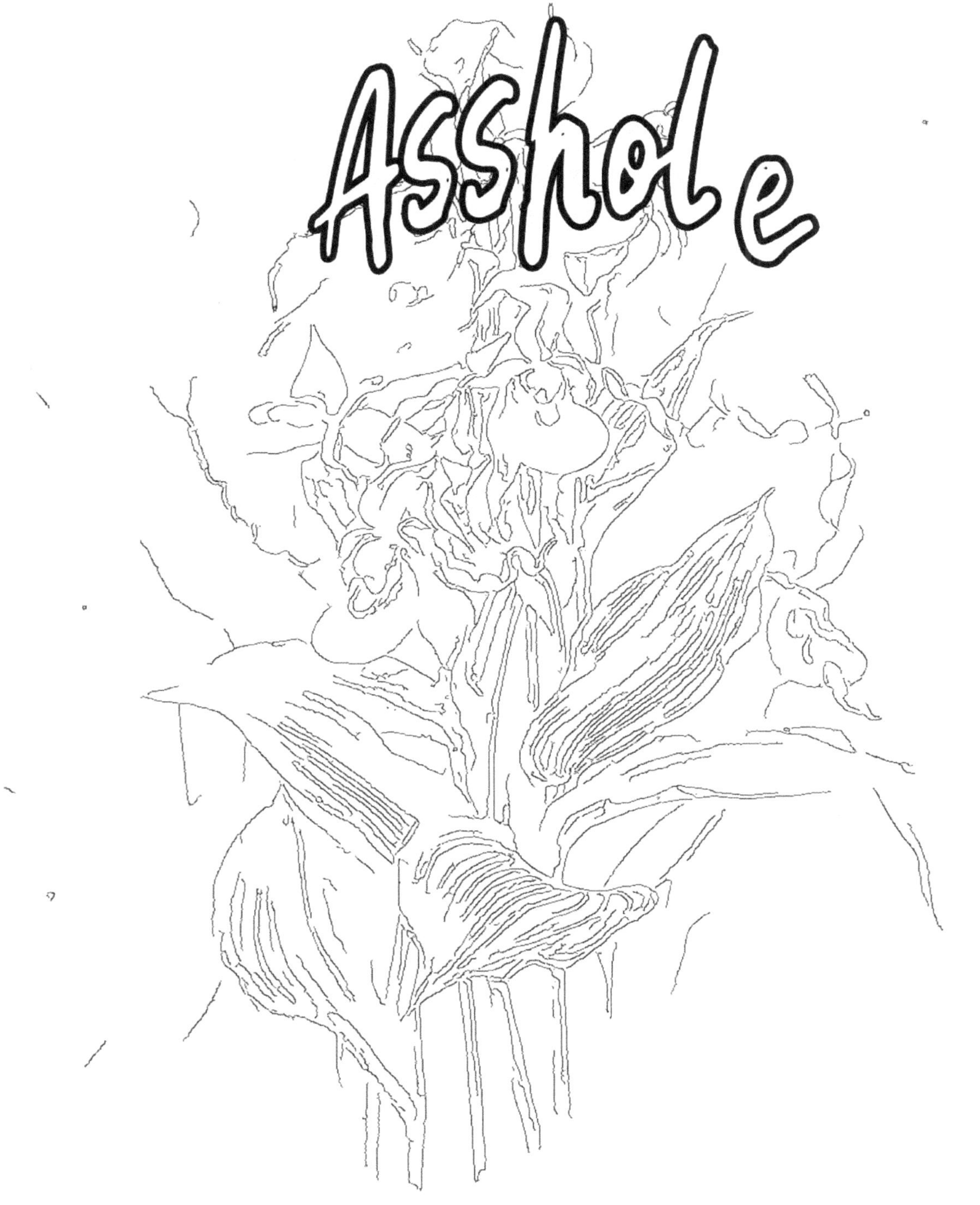
Asshole

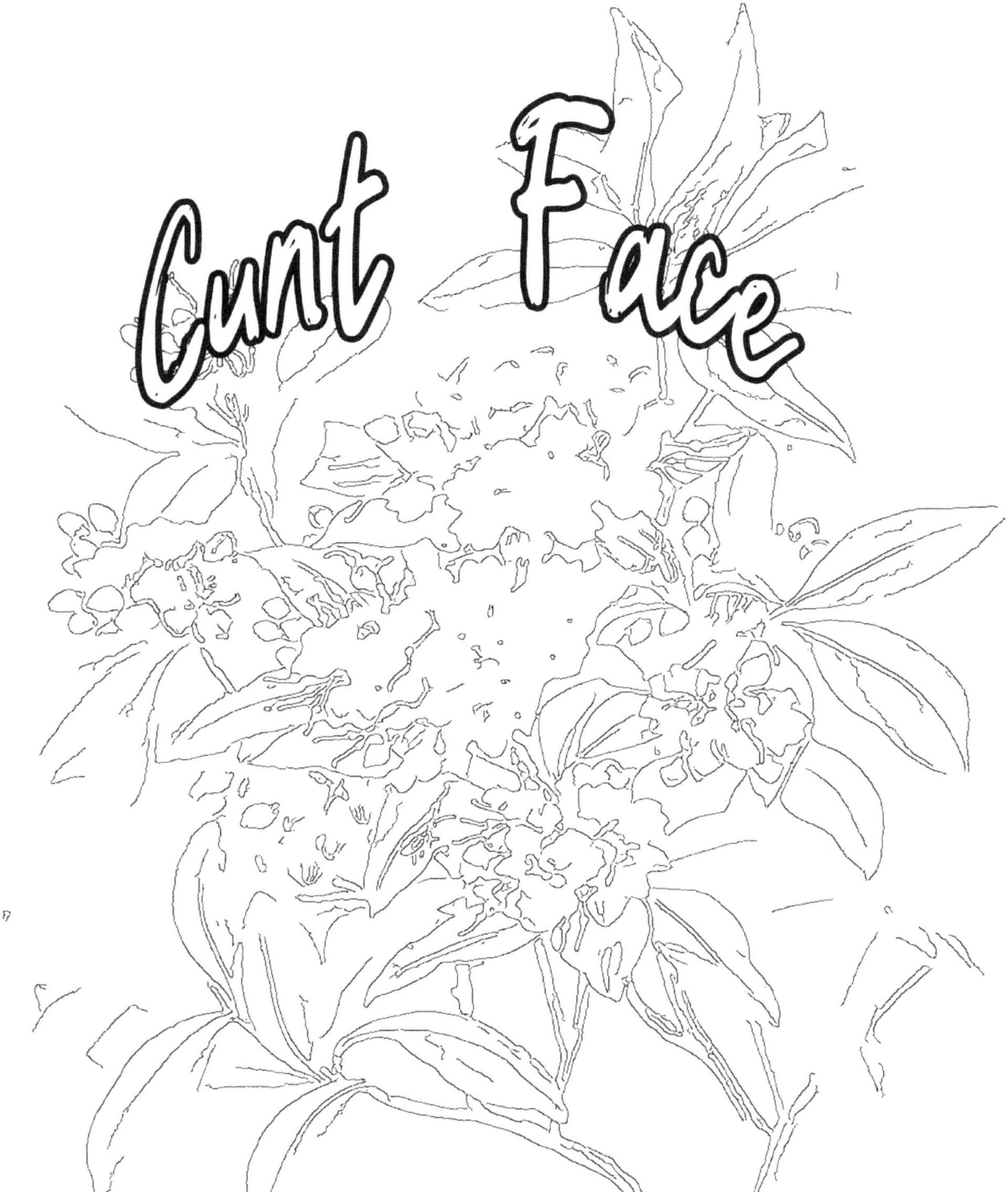
Cunt Face

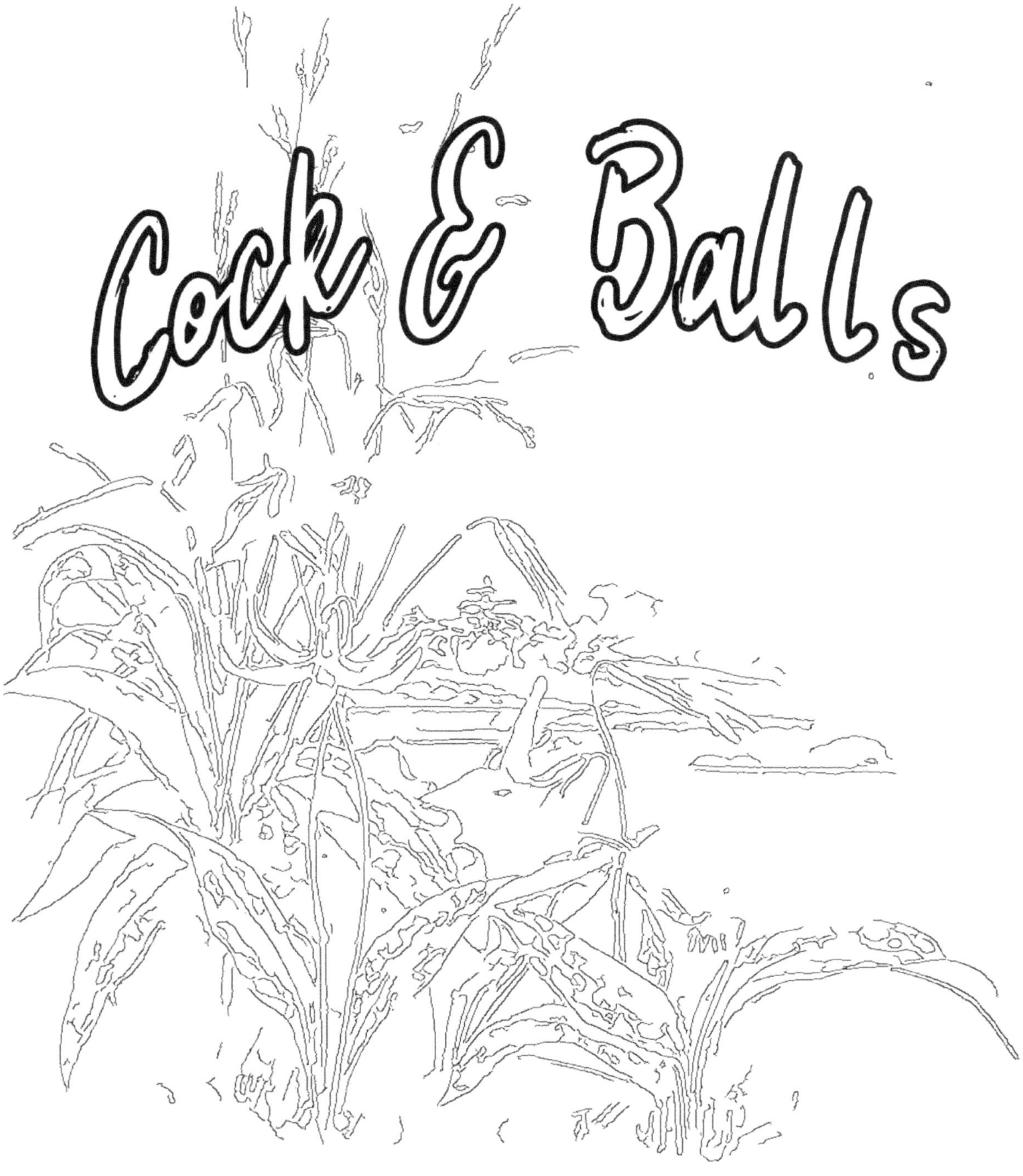
Cock & Balls

Bastard

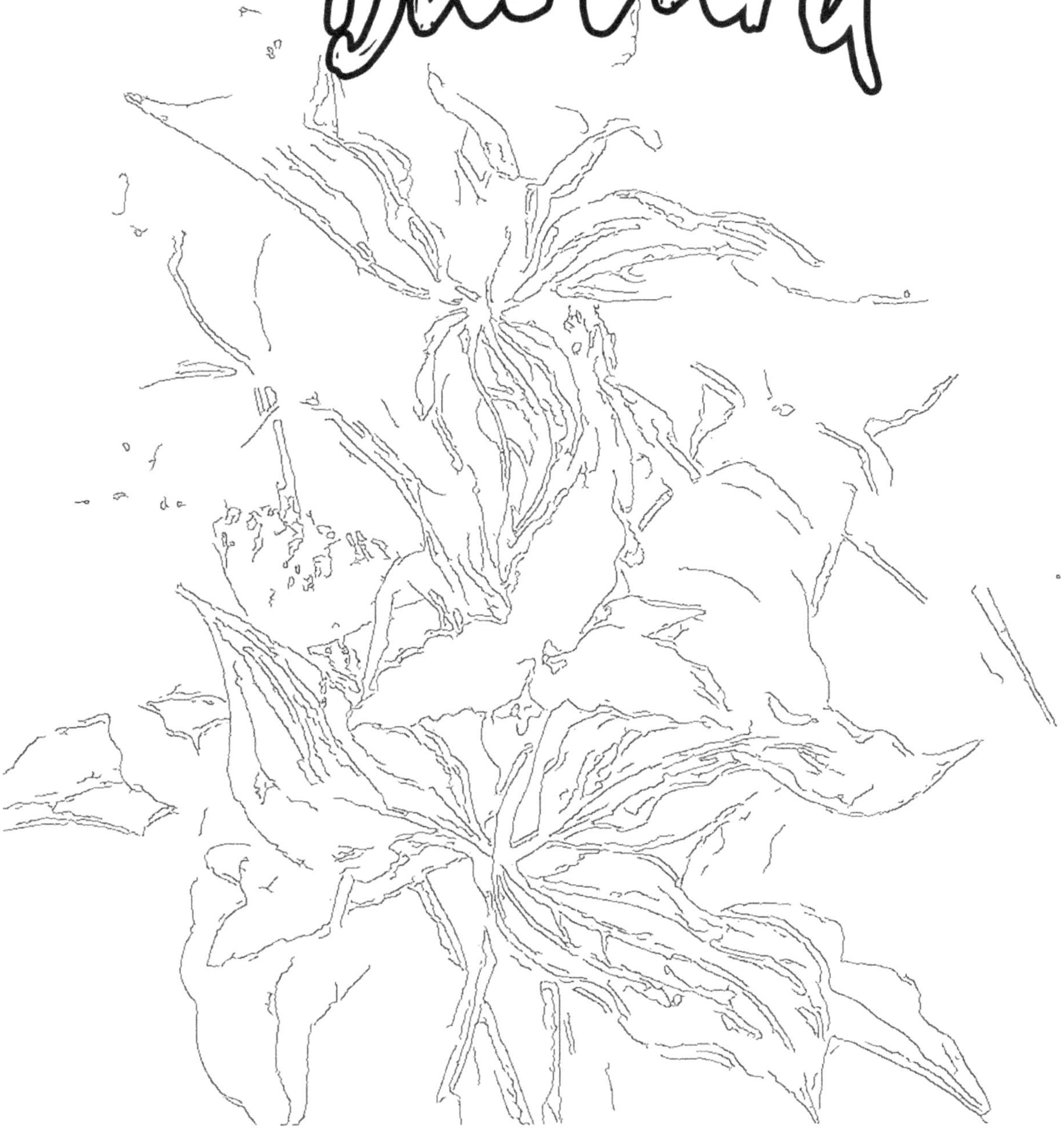

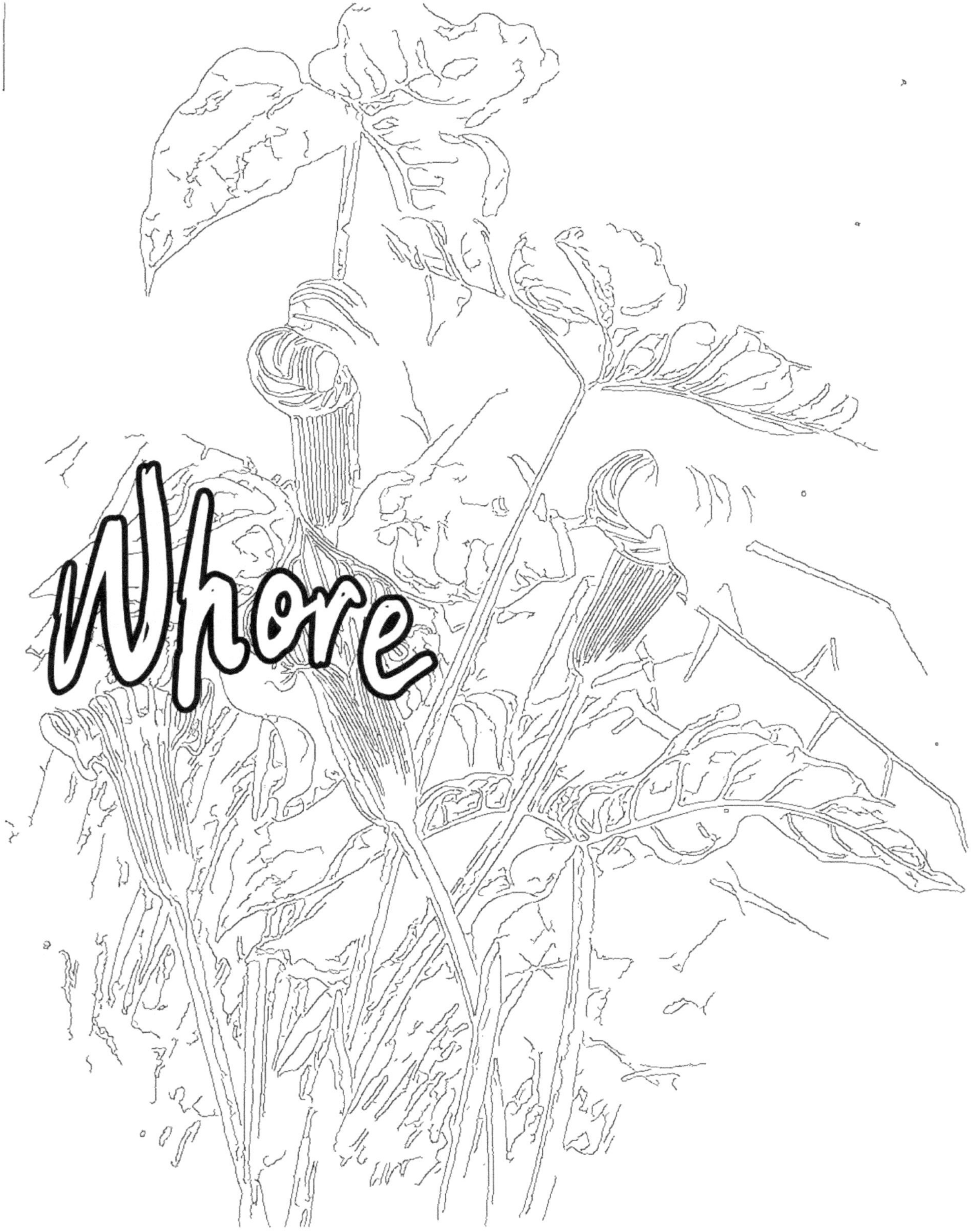
Whore

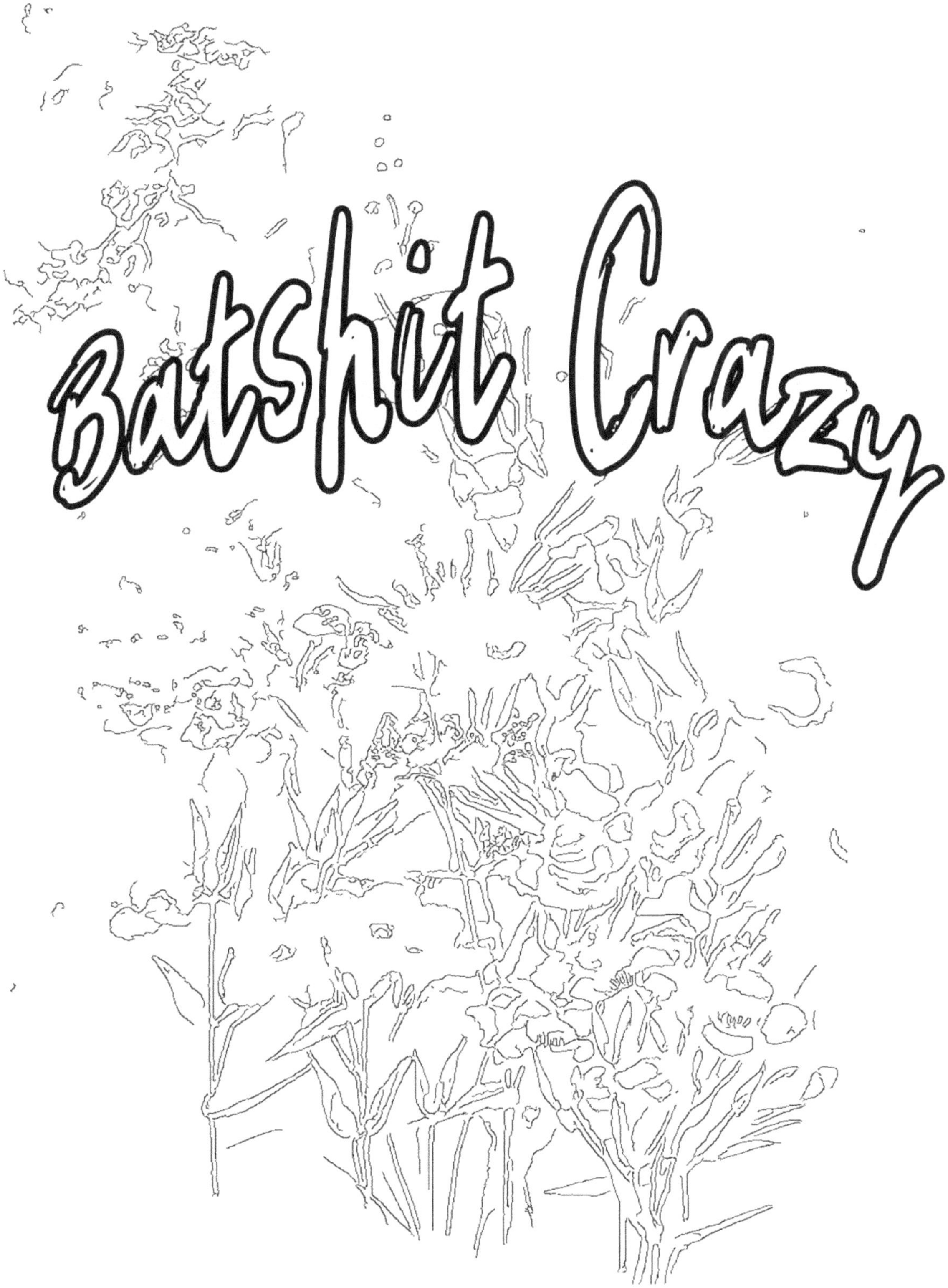
Batshit Crazy

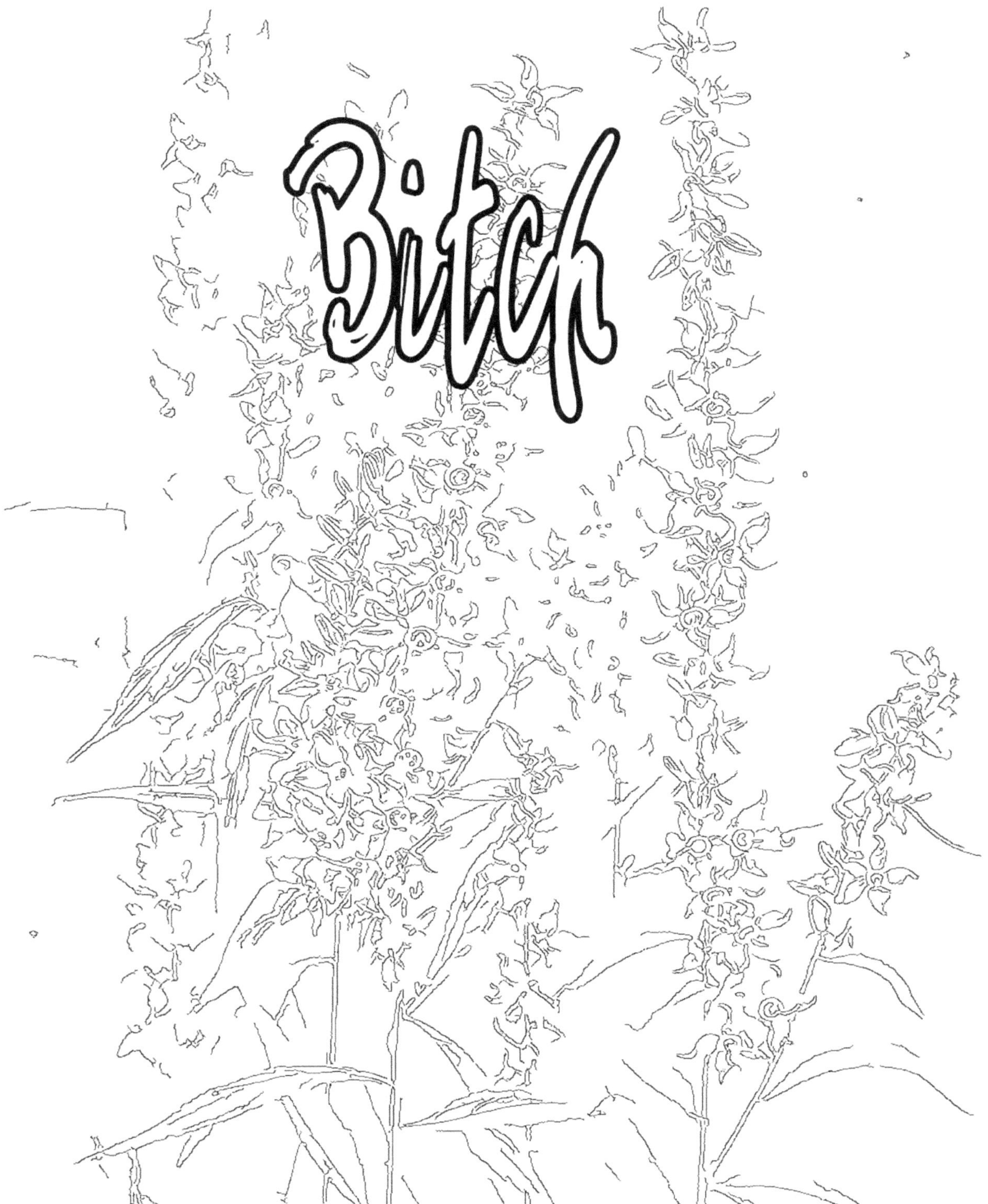
Bitch

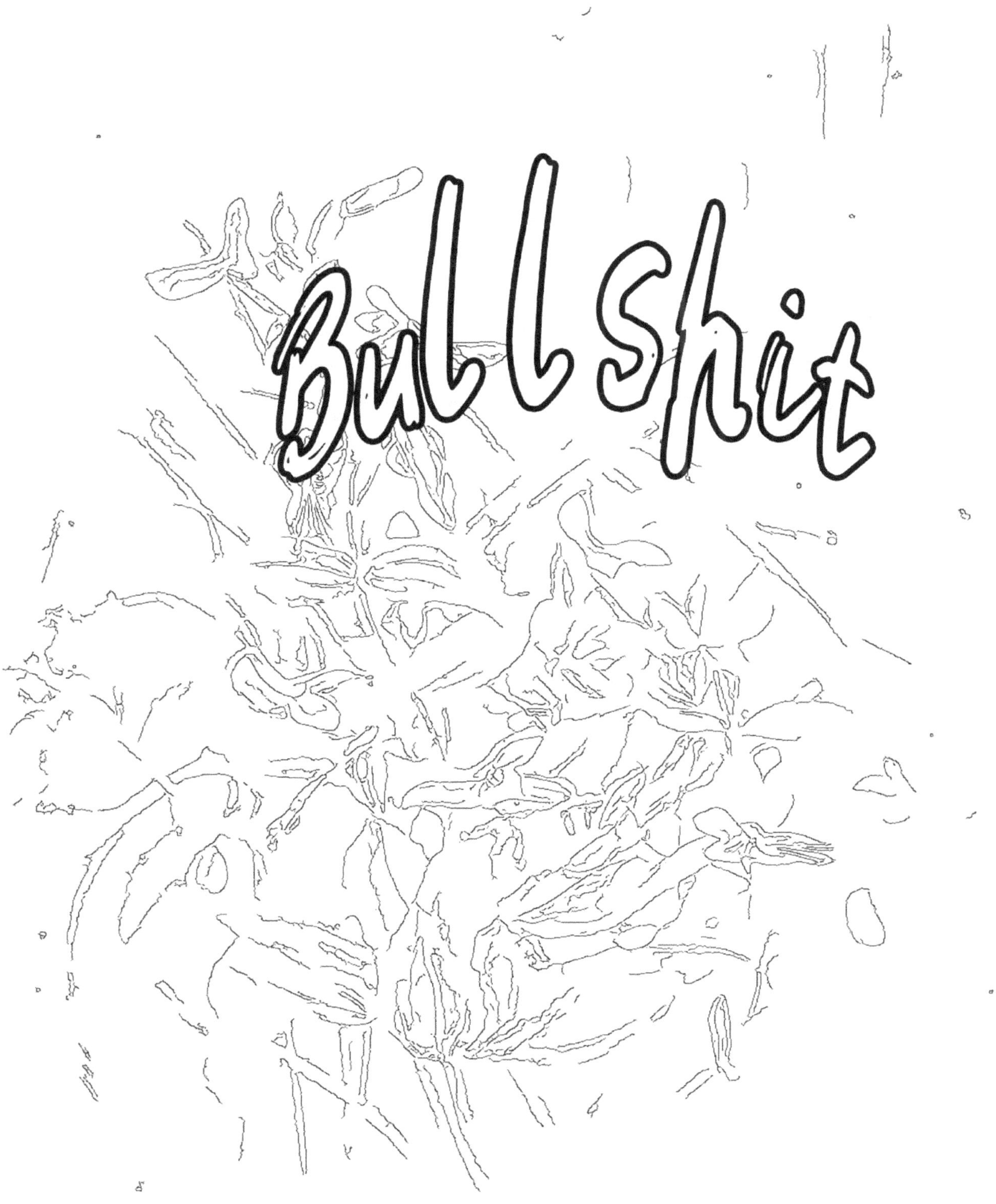
Bull Shit

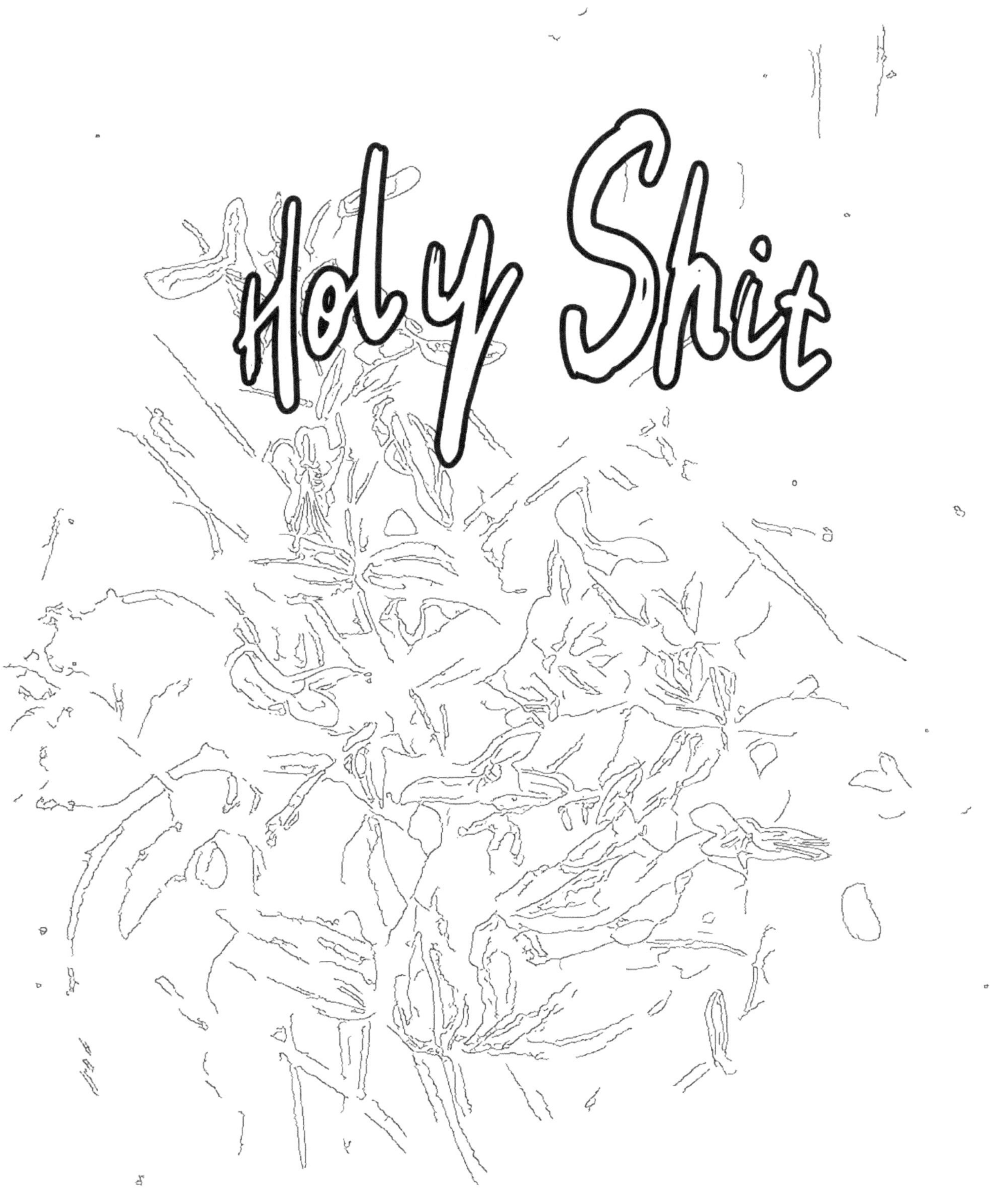
Holy Shit

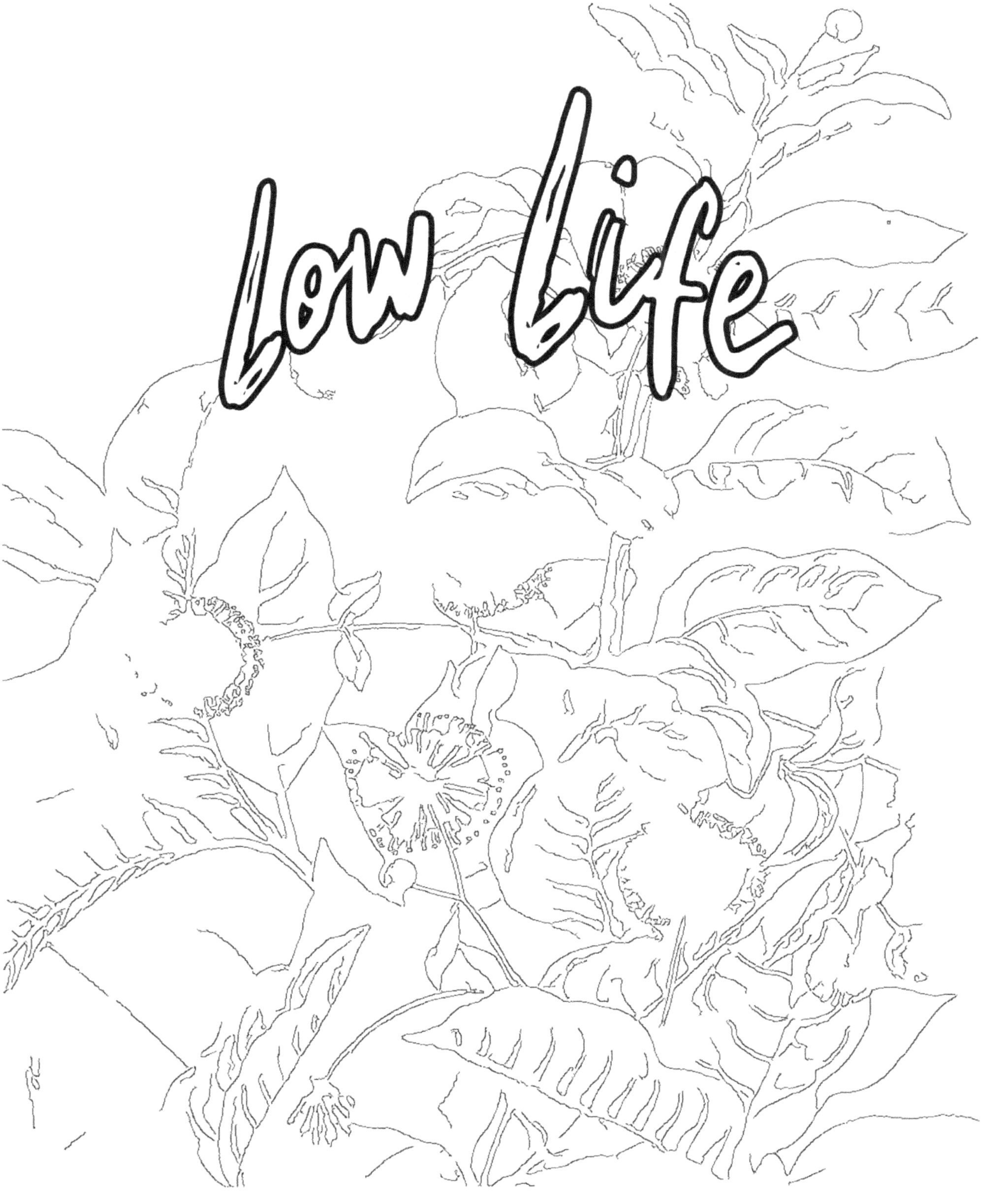
Low life

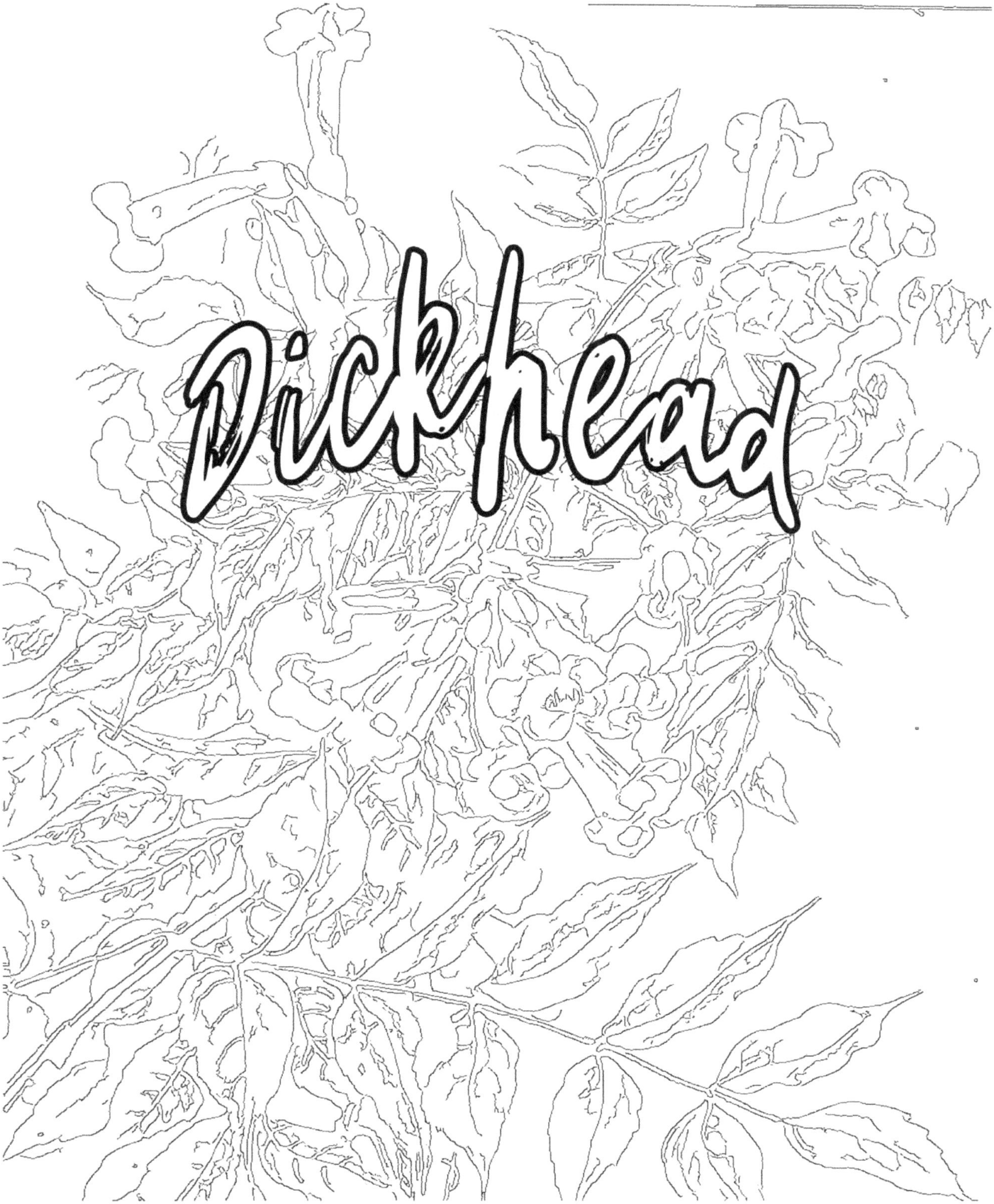
Dickhead

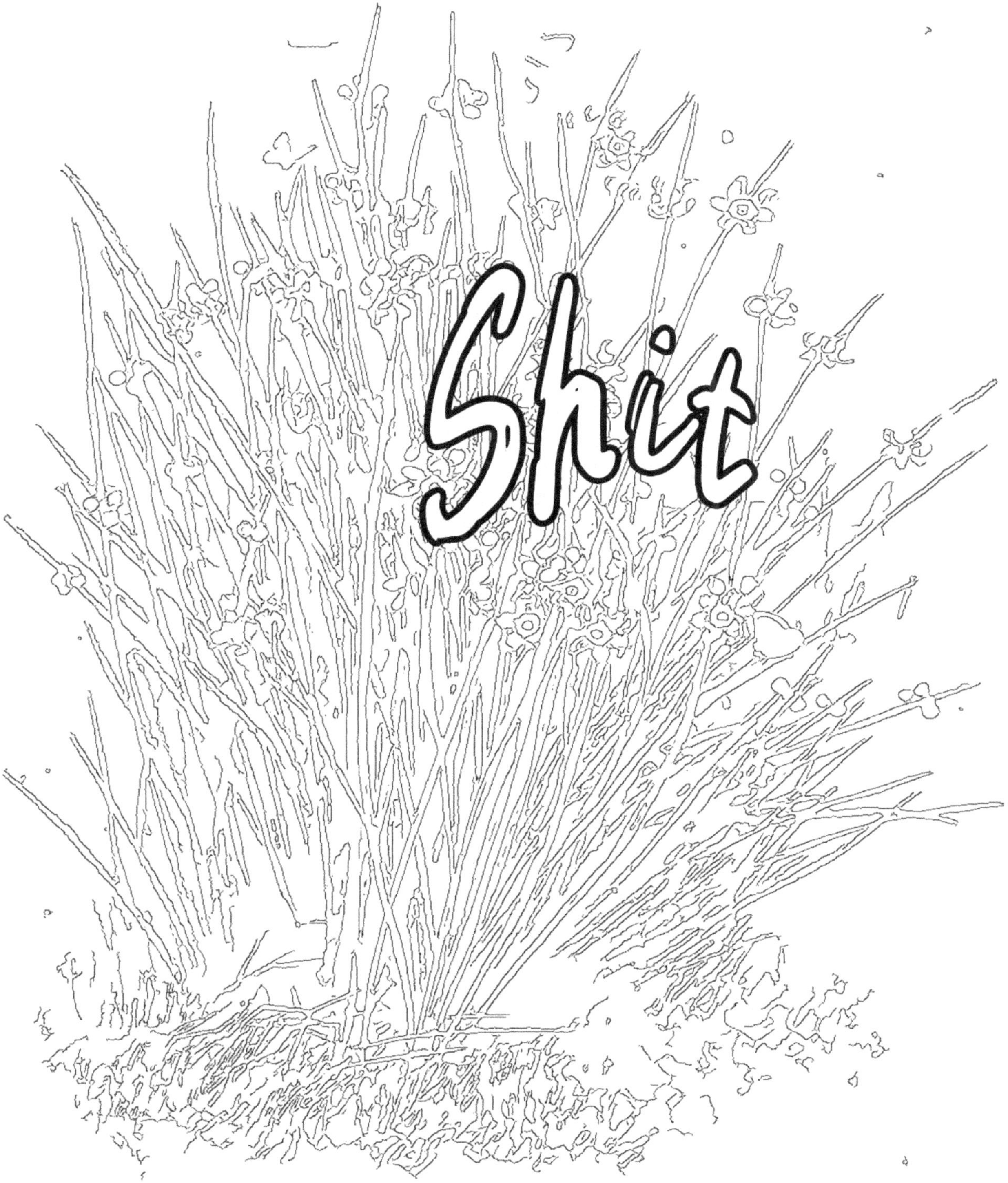
Shit

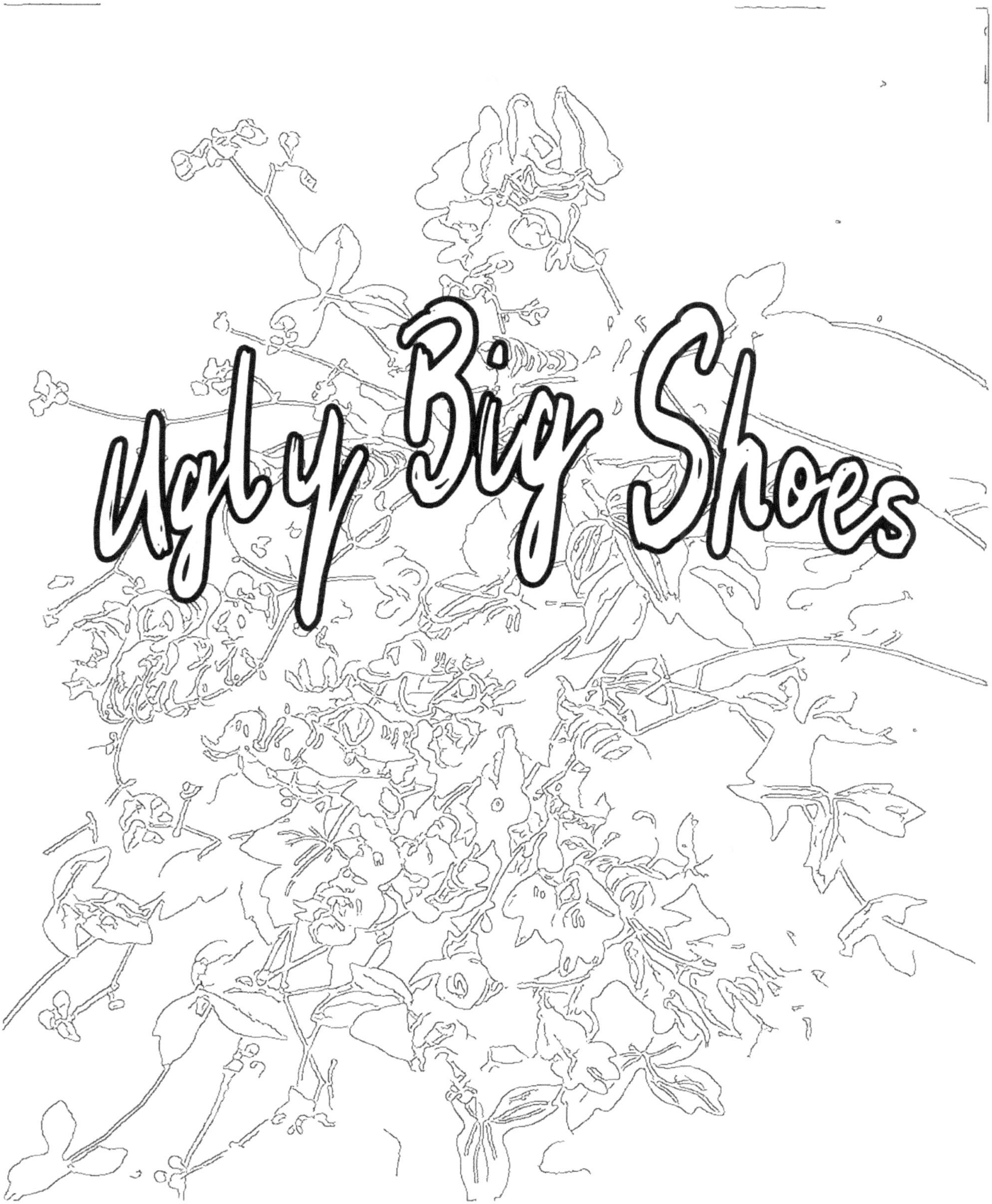
Ugly Big Shoes

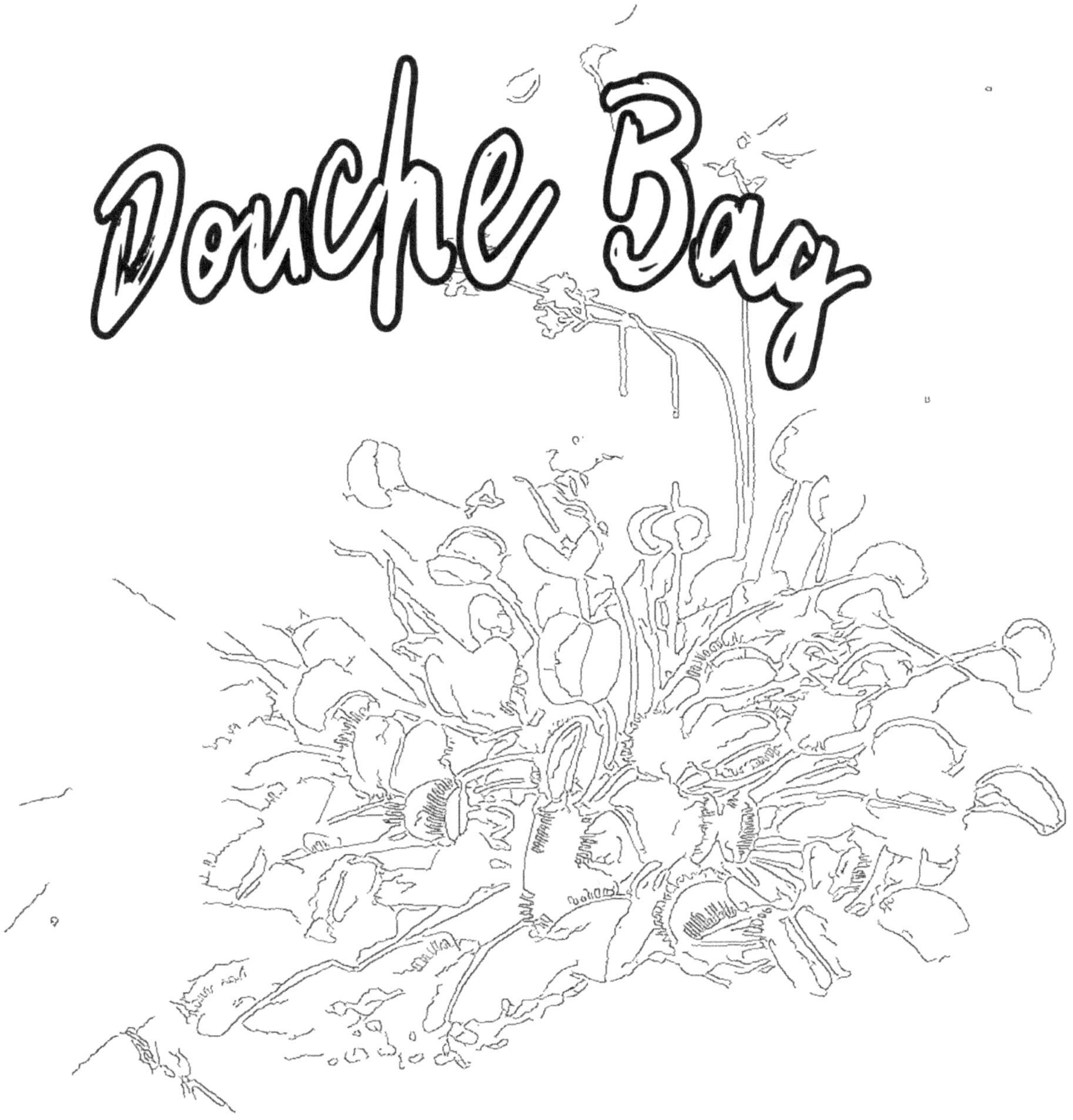
Douche Bag

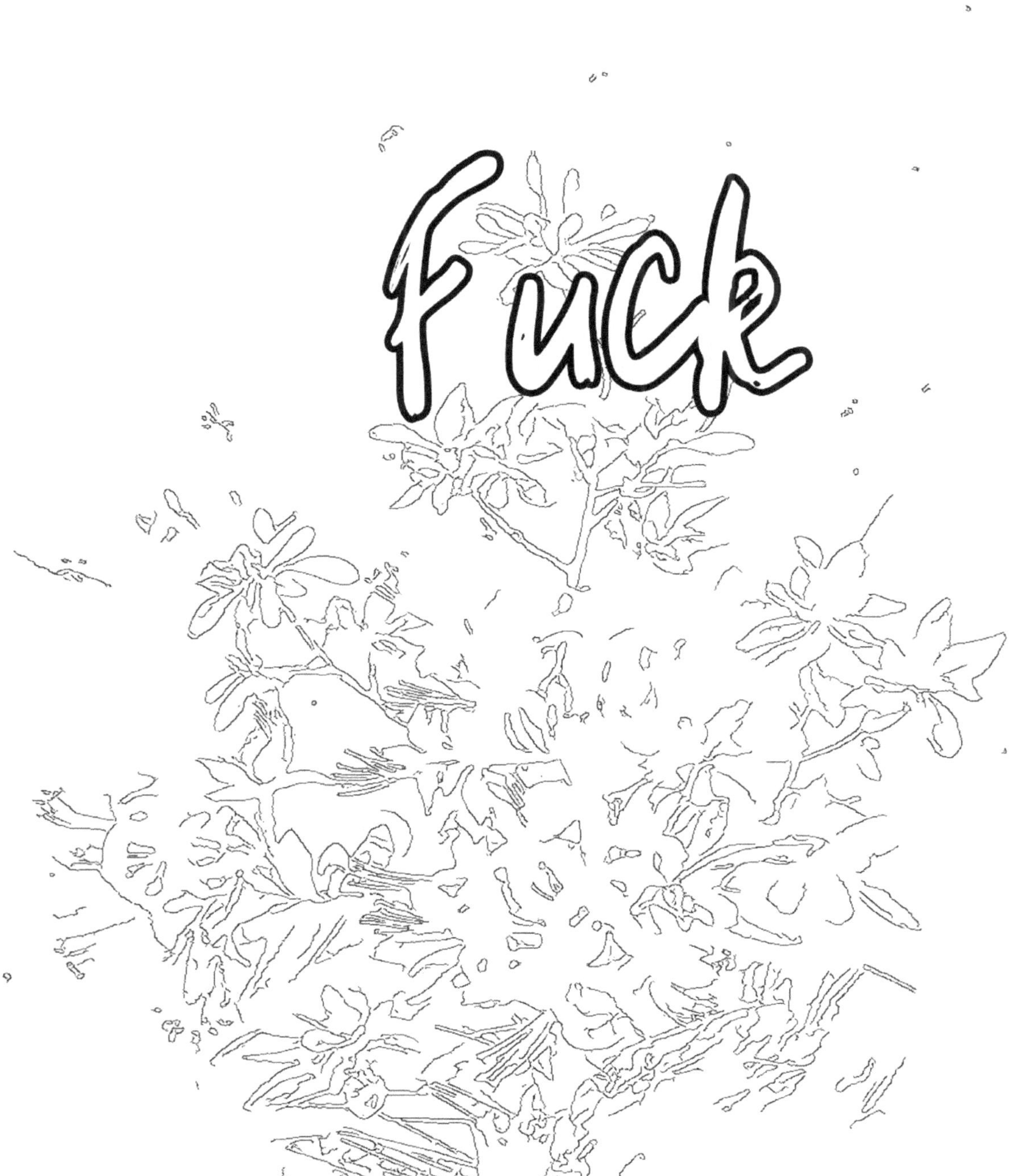
Fuck

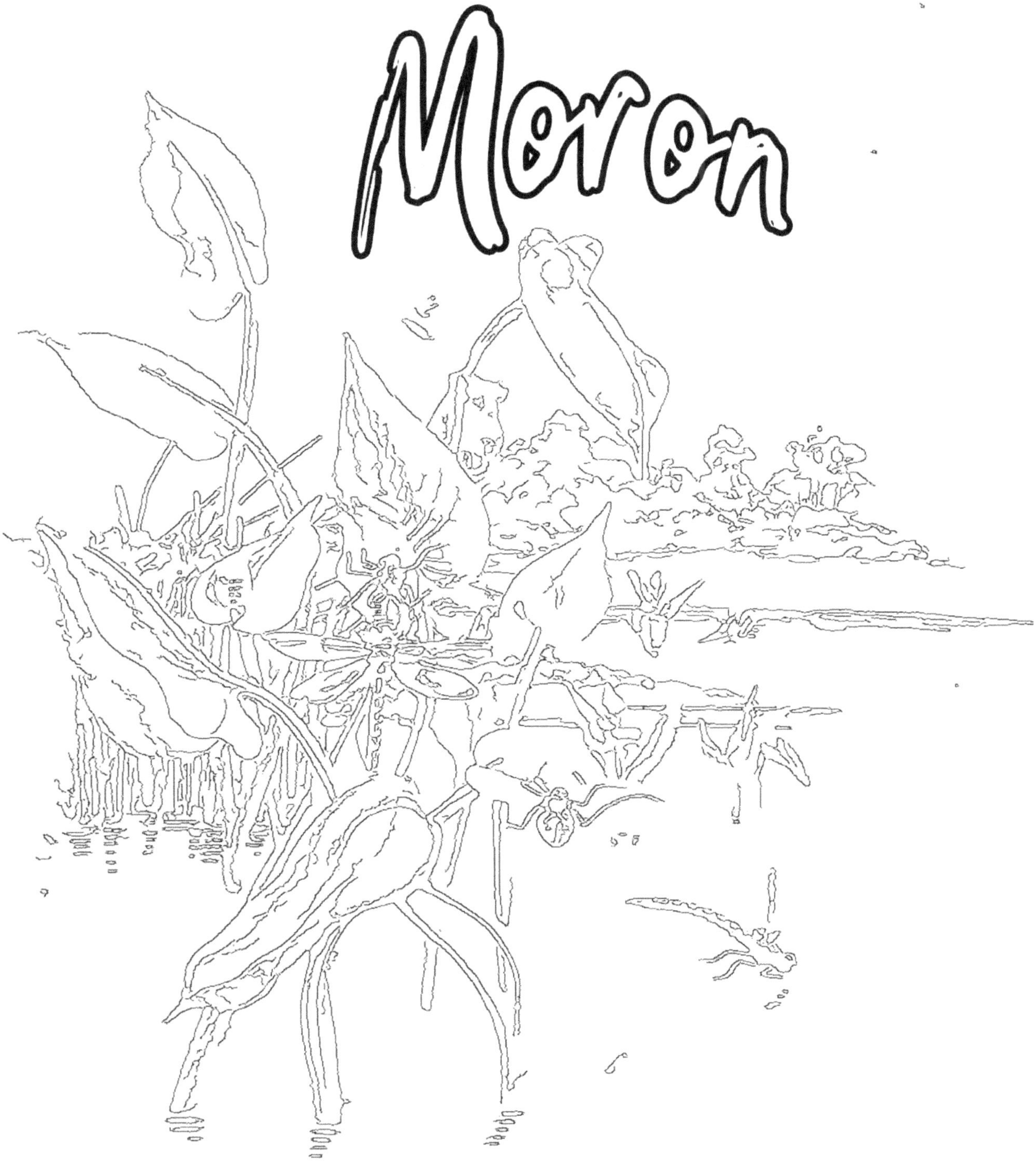
Moron

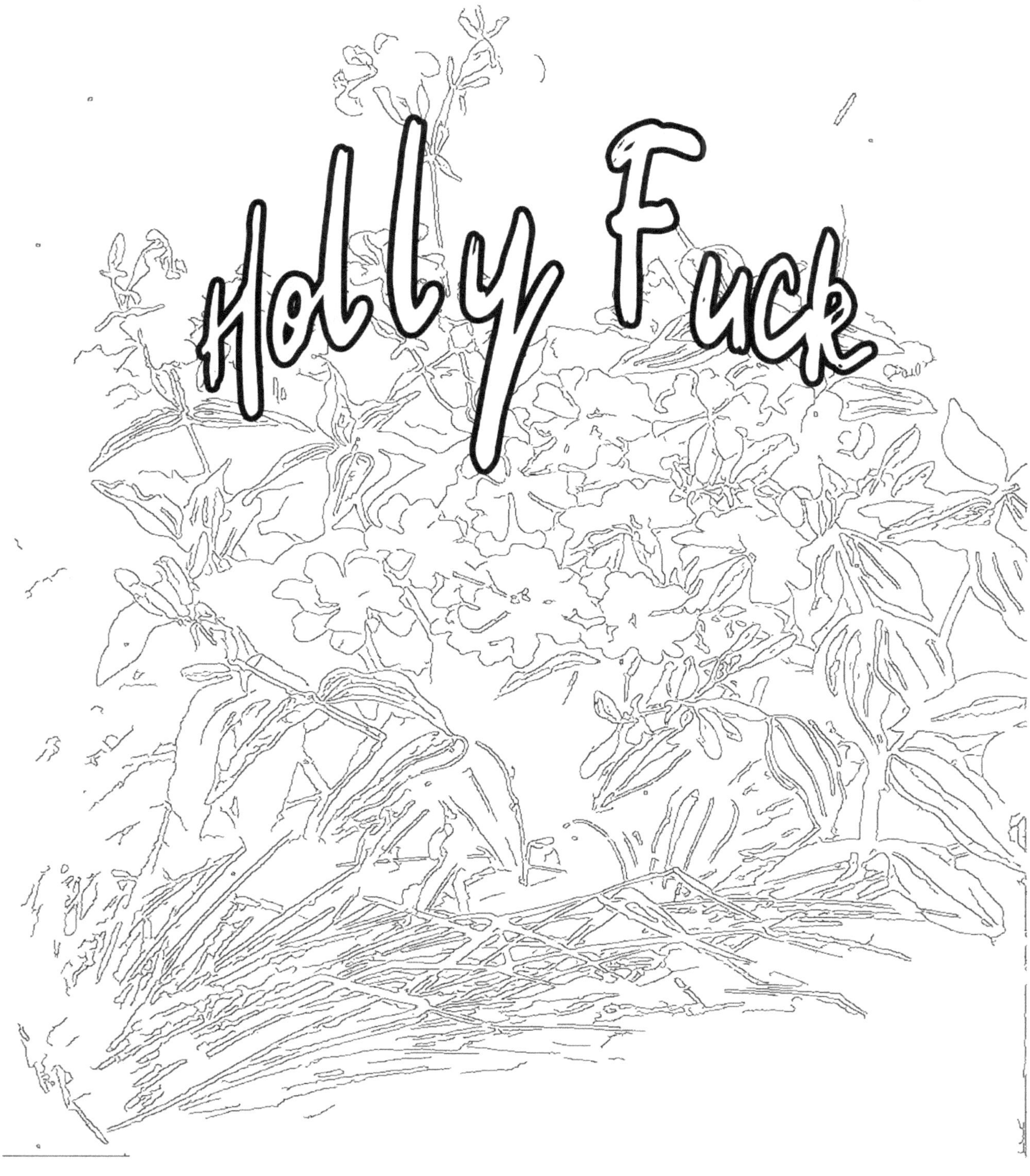
Holly Fuck

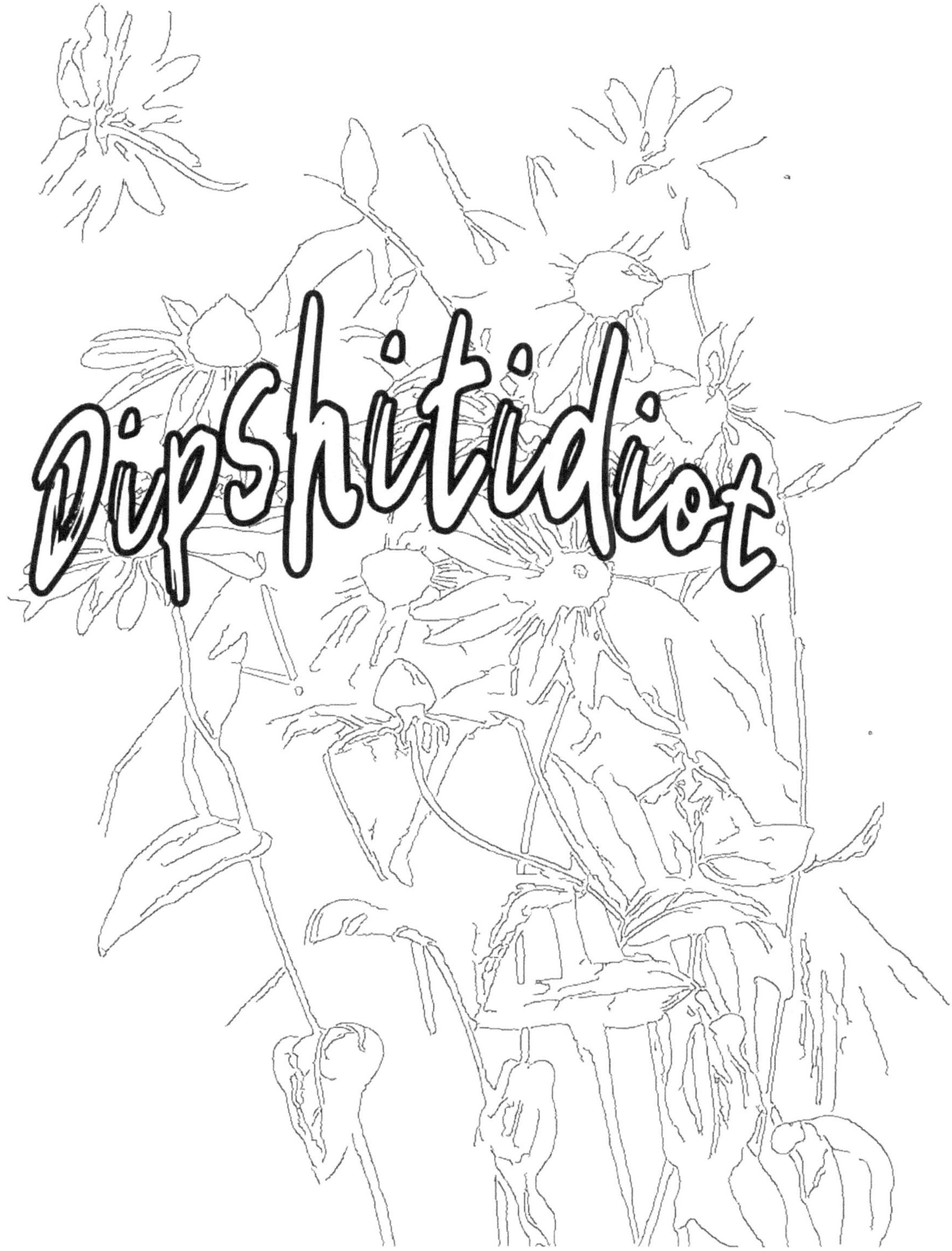
DipShitidiot

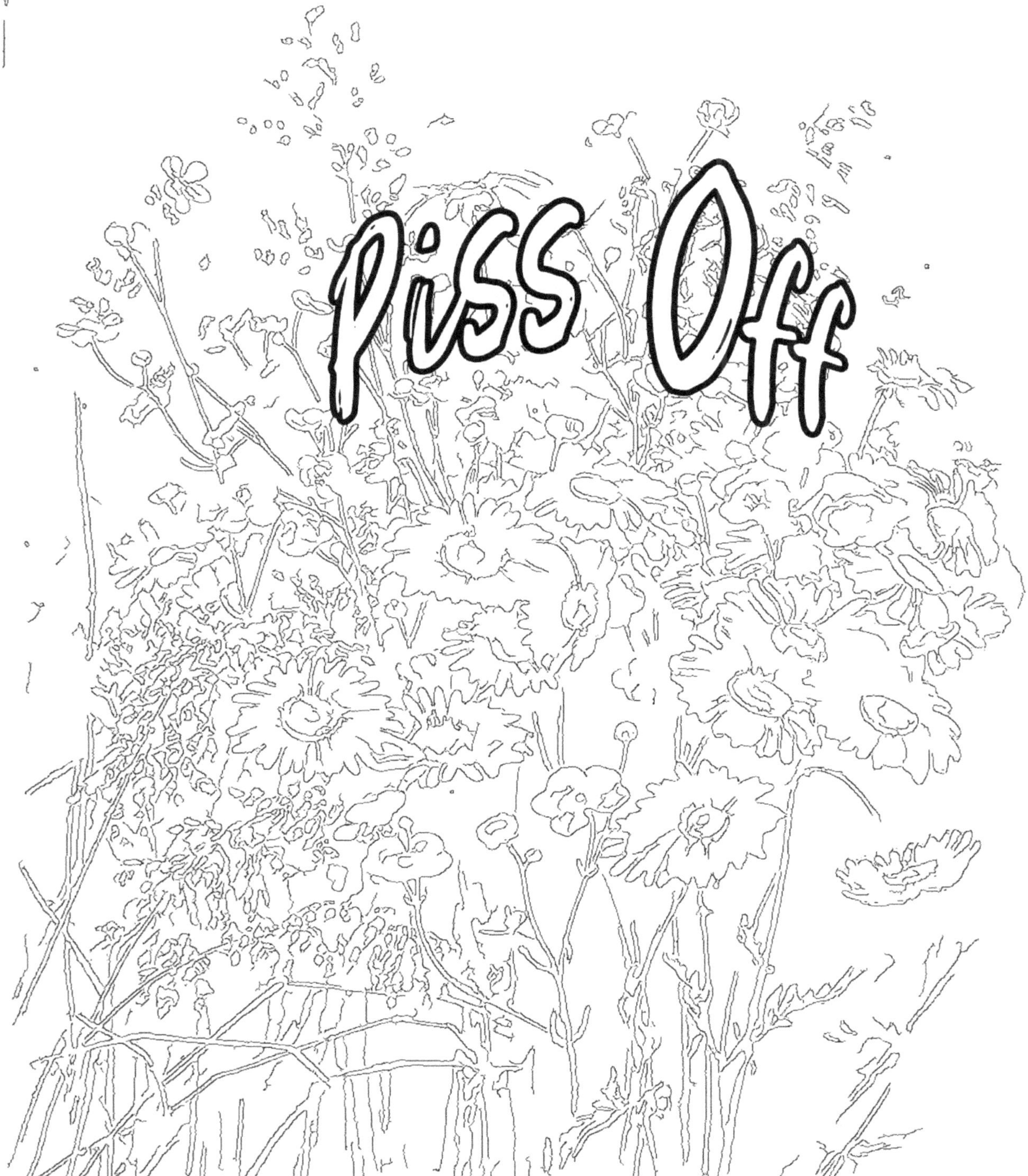
Piss Off

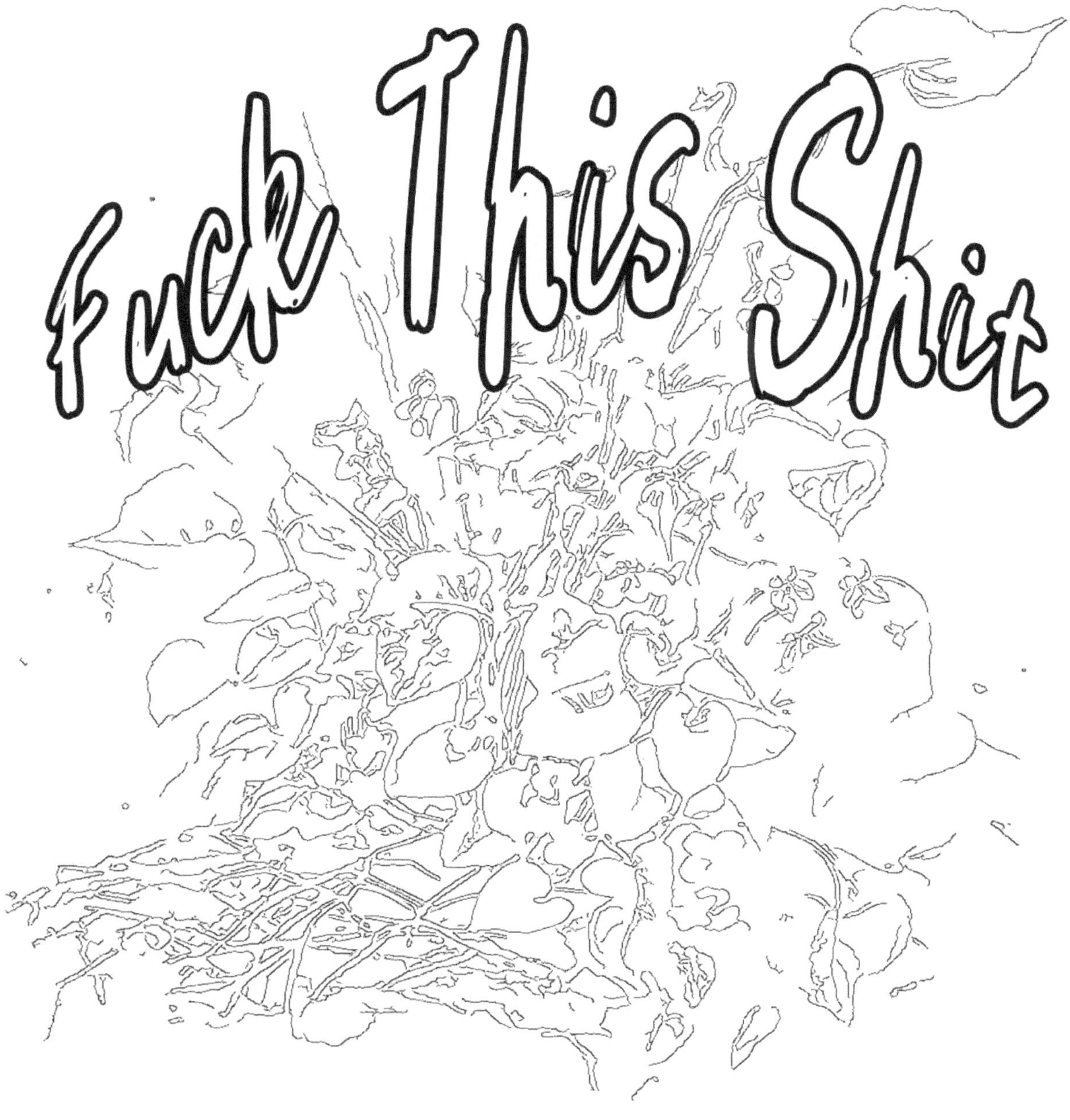
Fuck This Shit

Old Fart

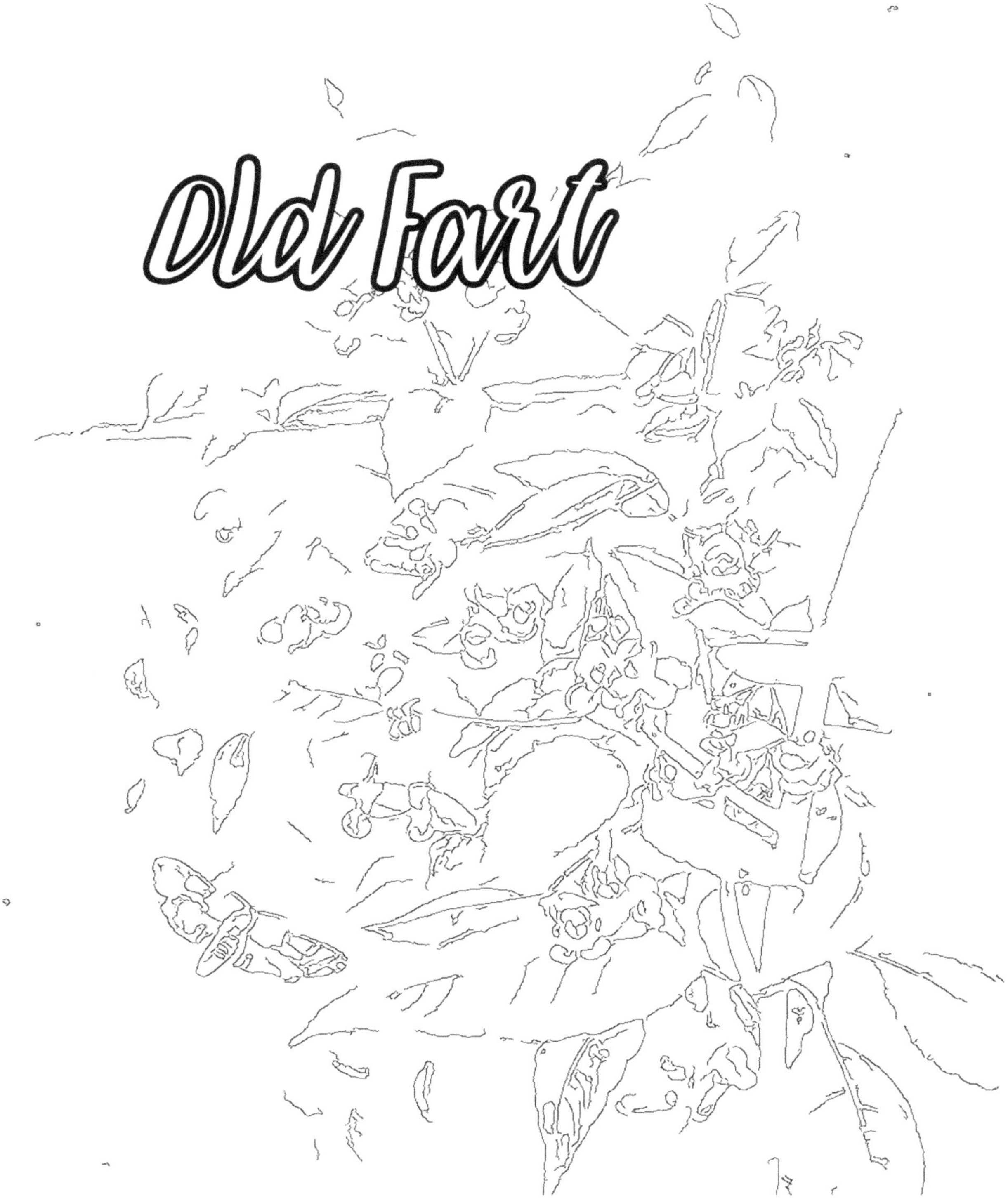

Attention Whore

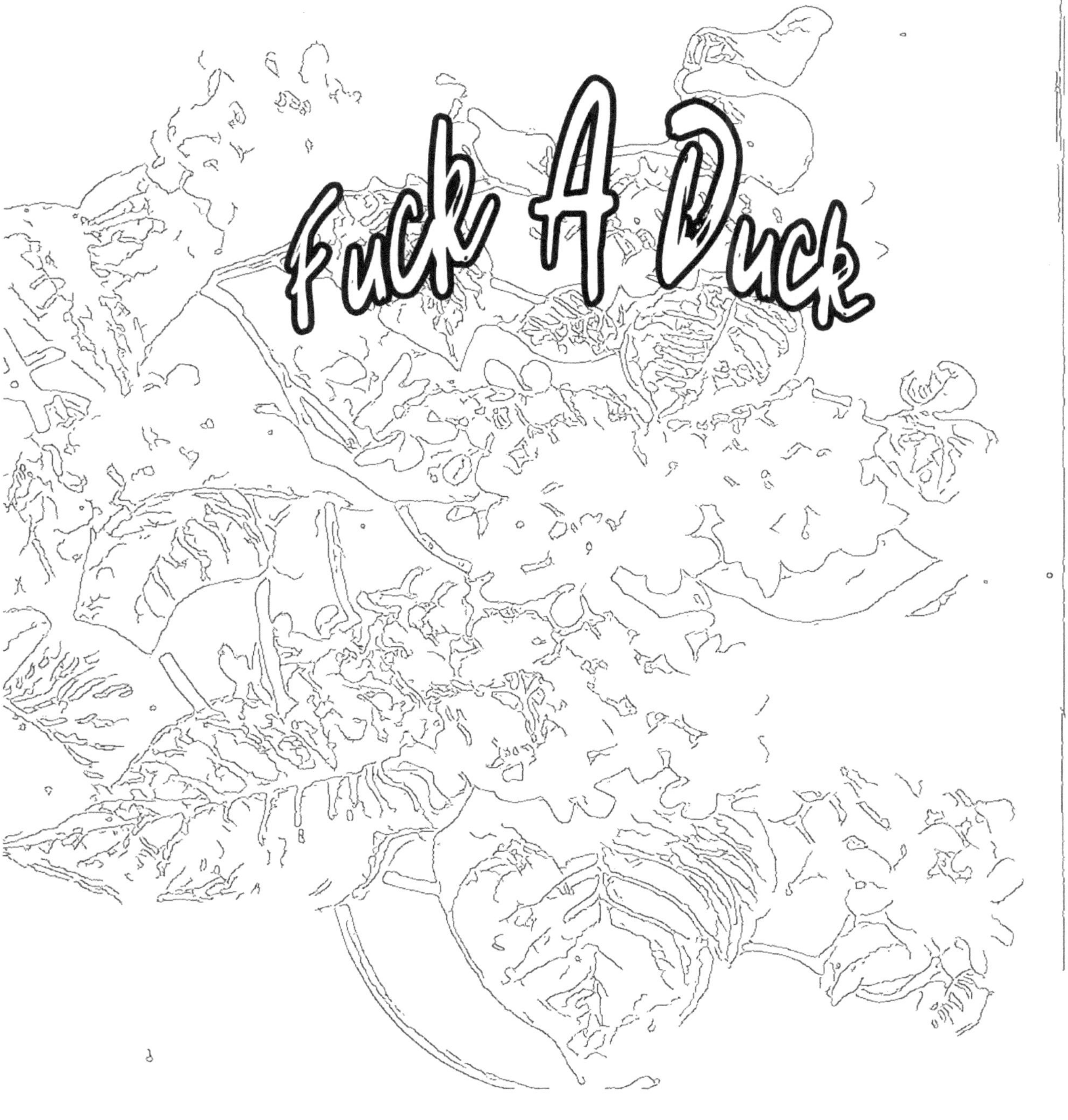
Fuck A Duck

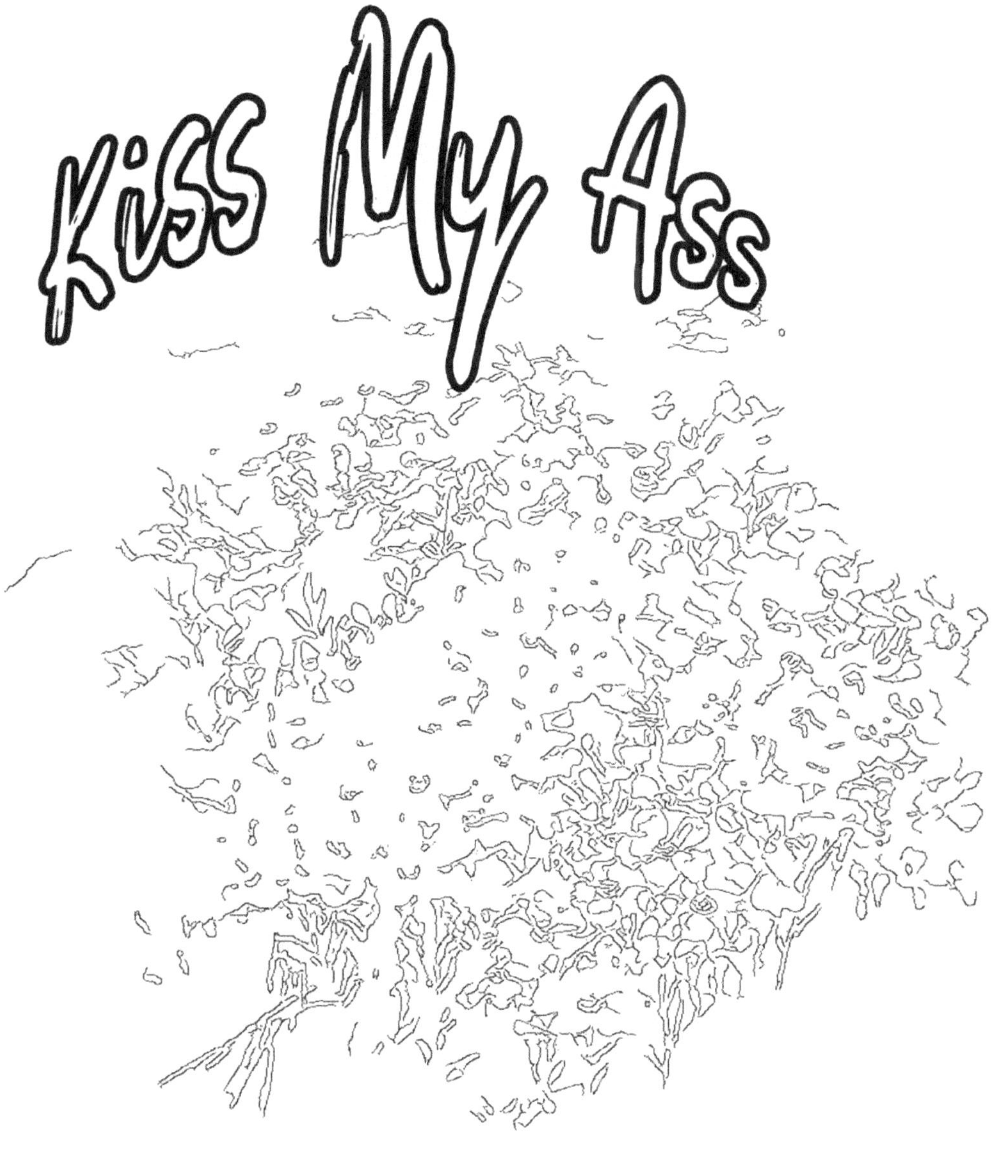
Kiss My Ass

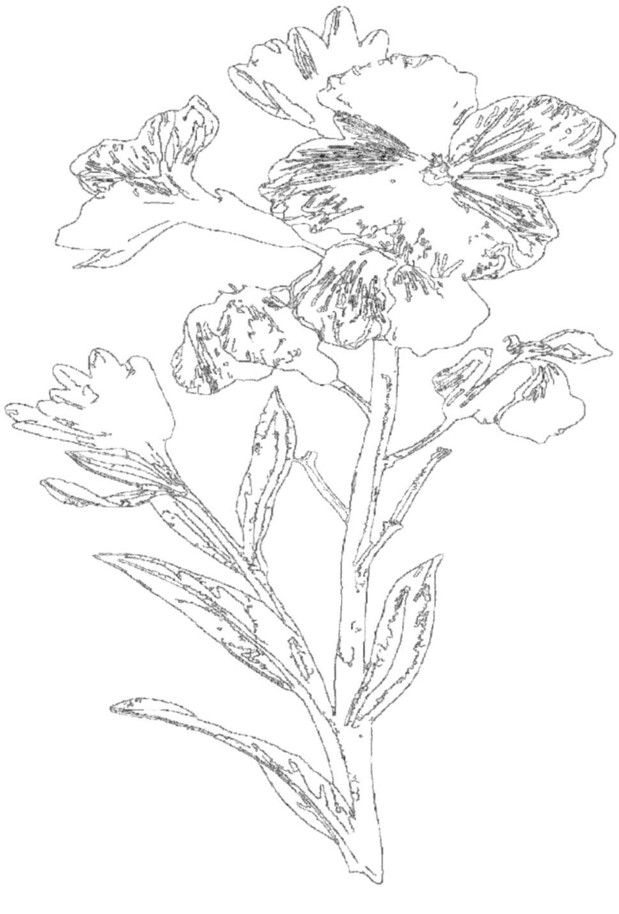

Have a good day.

www.ingramcontent.com/pod-product-compliance
Lightning Source LLC
Chambersburg PA
CBHW081620220526
45468CB00010B/2965
* 9 7 8 1 9 8 3 4 0 9 6 8 4 *